For your
anniversary
any anniversary

Mom

To Love One Another

To Love One Another

Poems Celebrating Marriage

Edited by Ginny Lowe Connors

Poetworks / Grayson Books

Published by Poetworks / Grayson Books
Post Office Box 270549
West Hartford, Connecticut 06127

Publisher's Cataloging-in-Publication
(Provided by Quality Books, Inc.)

To love one another : poems celebrating marriage / edited
   by Ginny Lowe Connors. – 1st ed.
   p. cm.
   LCCN 2001119169
   ISBN 0-9675554-3-4 (hardcover)
   ISBN 0-9675554-4-2 (softcover)

   1. Marriage – Poetry. 2. American poetry.
   I. Connors, Ginny Lowe.

   PS595.M3T65 2002   811'.540803543
                               QB101-701249

Library of Congress Catalog Card Number: 2001119169

For Marty

Table of Contents

Robert Hardy

Falling

for Ruth and Jason, August 23, 1997

You already know about love.
You fall in love. Falling is easy. Maybe you don't
see it coming. Maybe you brace yourself against the
wind in the door,
see the earth circling below
and jump. Falling is easy. It feels like flight.
You feel your kinship with clouds, with light,
stuff of stars, atoms that float and fall,
meteors, stars that still glow
with the start of everything.
You raise your arms like wings. Butterfly
or belly-flop. You feel the earth expanding –
don't look down. Reach for the cord.
Falling is easy. But is this love
or gravity? Pull the cord. Yes –
love blossoms from the weight you carry,
the question, the tug at your heart.
The parachute pops like a cork.
Now you float in the arms of the atmosphere,
milkweed floss, dandelion seed,
no longer afraid to take root in the earth –
but still floating a while, ecstasy and trust, your
          high-
altitude heart settling back into a steadier beat,
the tilt of the earth, seasons and days.
But here you are floating – buoyed by invitations
and arrangements. Now you look down.
The ground looms like a date, circled for landing.

Robert Hardy

The fields look like RSVPs. Your feet touch. The parachute
falls around you like a wedding dress.
You've landed together. Dance while the earth steadies
beneath your feet. Hold each other up.
Now you will walk together into ordinary days.
Your parachute may become a maternity dress, a mortgage,
a tissue for your tears. It may be divided into diapers,
waterproof sheets, a layette, stories to tell your grandchildren.
Days may come when you forget how it felt to float.
But still this moment of landing lives inside you,
when the touch of the ground felt like a vow –
I will always be there. I will catch you if you fall.

Fran Portley

Heart Over Head

I can't explain
what I don't understand.
My granddaughter tells me
to live in the real world,
but mine is lovelier.
This April afternoon pear trees
stand like brides, songbirds sing
mating songs and children toss
crumbs to swans swimming two by two
in your town's park. I sit here
in my lavender skirt hoping
to know your children and
everything, everything about you.
Call it ridiculous,
totally foolish, I will agree.
Nevertheless I'm completely
heart over head
magically, sweetly, in love!

Mike Wiegard

If Thou Wouldst

I offer thee my hand in love, to hold
Thy heart so carefully, to understand
With every touch; my fingers to enfold
Forever thine, if thou wouldst take my hand.
I pledge to thee my vow of love, my heart
Is thine, mine eyes for thine alone, for thou
Hast my devotion – faithful and stalwart,
Eternal, true – if thou wouldst give thy vow.
I give to thee this ring with love. The sun
Of my heart's new dawn doth rise, shimmering
Within, for thee, my soul's full moon, the one
I wouldst betroth, if thou wouldst wear this ring.
My love, in thee my dreams, my hopes reside,
I humbly ask thee: wouldst thou be my bride?

Shoshauna Shy

I Know Wichita, Kansas

for I was on flight 91
coming in for a landing
when someone asked will you marry me,
the trees below us as fake as those trees
architects make with sponge

Both of us were giddy with shock
that he popped the question
and that I yessed back instantly
unwise to what this yes would mean
in the next five seconds

No carnival, no symphony
no event at our destination
would hold a candle to this sensation:
Hearts soaring like bottle rockets
while dropping 300 feet

It was like dancing inside
a kaleidoscope while cresting
the peak on a roller coaster the day
your team meets the state champion
and races home with the trophy

I know Wichita, Kansas
in a way that nobody else does
for I was flying into its arms
when someone asked will you marry me

Alice Friman

The Wedding Poem

This day
Let no one claim
That love is false. Let no one
Tell a tale of Love's dilution,
Cross his lips with doubt,
Or discuss the up and down and up
Of Love chained to a balance beam –
Laundry and who takes out the trash.

Instead, let us make a pact:
To stop for this short time
The radio in our heads, the voices
Of discontent that drive us mad –
The committee of shoulds and oughts
And might have beens. The old harangue
Of never never never.
To forsake, for these next minutes
(Not for this couple but for ourselves),
All the symptoms of our days.

Alice Friman

Then, together, let us swear,
That this sun, this sky, these vows,
This bubble balanced on the point
Of a knife is all there is –
For we have pushed aside the walls
That close us in
To come to this shared space. And see –
We have filled the space with flowers,
Where Love, like some bright bird
Too swift to hold,
May light for us a while and sing.

X. J. Kennedy

For a Wedding in a Week of Devastation

to Charles Christensen and
Elizabeth Marquand Welch

You choose each other and you choose this day.
After days dark with nightmares we'd forget,
The sun shall come, to hold triumphant sway.

Despite dust clouds that shroud us, huge and gray,
Billowing from each television set,
You choose each other and you choose today,

And choosing so, you toss dull dread away
Like some lost memory of an old regret,
Preferring that the sun come, to hold sway.

Might you have chosen reasons to delay
This glad exchange of promises? And yet
You chose each other and you chose today.

Those who chose sudden death have had their day
But you choose life. Let it continue, let
The veil be lifted, let the sun hold sway

Though clouds may shadow it. Clouds drift away.
Your love leaves us who love you in your debt.
You choose each other and you choose this day.
The sun shall come, to hold triumphant sway.

Krista Clercx

Wedding Day

"How can we know the dancer from the dance?"
– William Butler Yeats

You are the feet that make it move.
You are the music that makes it smooth.
You are the arms that make it last.
You are the dance and the dancers,
the ones who love and the love others envy.
You are each other

in the way you might finish each other's sentences
or think of an early morning conversation
in spare moments at the office,
the way you know the other is in the room without
    speaking.
You know how he brushes his teeth,
how she wakes up during thunderstorms,
how he reads the newspaper before dinner,
how she moves her hair to answer the phone.

People pass you when you're driving together.
They know you are each other –
the way you talk about a vacation or the groceries
or what you'll do to the kitchen next summer.
They notice how you lean toward each other,
how your eyes pull each other closer.

Krista Clercx

You know each other and you know the ordinary
    days
are the ones that make you intimate and blessed.
You are each other,
sometimes stepping on toes as you move across the
    floor,
but returning to twirl gracefully on the tip of a
    finger.
The music floats past your heart and into your soul.
You know the dance and you dance it.

Marge Piercy

The Chuppah

The chuppah stands on four poles.
The home has its four corners.
The chuppah stands on four poles.
The marriage stands on four legs.
Four points loose the winds
that blow on the walls of the house,
the south wind that brings the cold rain,
the north wind that brings the cold sun
and the snow, the long west wind
bringing the weather off the far plains.

Here we live open to the seasons.
Here the winds caress and cuff us
contrary and fierce as bears.
Here the winds are caught and snarling
in the pines, a cat in a net clawing
breaking twigs to fight loose.
Here the winds brush your face
soft in the morning as feathers
that float down from a dove's breast.
Here the moon sails up out of the ocean
dripping like a just washed apple.
Here the sun wakes us like a baby.
Therefore the chuppah has no sides.

Marge Piercy

It is not a box.
It is not a coffin.
It is not a dead end.
Therefore the chuppah has no walls.
We have made a home together
open to the weather of our time.
We are mills that turn in the winds of struggle
converting fierce energy into bread.

This canopy is the cloth of our table
where we share fruit and vegetables
of our labor, where our care for the earth
comes back and we take its body in ours.

The canopy is the cover of our bed
where our bodies open their portals wide,
where we eat and drink the blood
of our love, where the skin shines red
as a swallowed sunrise and we burn
in one furnace of joy molten as steel
and the dream is flesh and flower.

Marge Piercy

O my love O my love we dance
under the chuppah standing over us
like an animal on its four legs,
like a table on which we set our love
for a feast, like a tent
under which we work
not safe but no longer solitary
in the searing heart of our time.

Andrea Hollander Budy

Wedding Poem

beginning with a line by Edna St. Vincent Millay

You are more than half of all I am.
This face you see, these eyes, my solid, shaky hands
     are merely
tools to hold my gaze upon you deeply as I can.

Before today our friends and family saw us
     separately, our plans
to marry no more than an expert's setting of two
     jewels
into a single ring, half of which is more than half of
     all I am

Before we met, my life was fine enough. I could
     stand
the busy work days, the weekends filling up with
     more than
I could hold. Today I gaze upon you deeply as I
     can

and I am filled. I look into your eyes and try to see
     in them
what I cannot see but somehow know: myself full
because of you, and you more than half of all I am.

Two people marrying is nothing new. I am
lucky to find music for my words. I know we
     cannot lose
what we hold if we gaze as deeply as we can

and – most important – if we do not stop. Today
    we claim
aloud our promises, our insistent love, which is
    more than an impulse
to hold our gaze upon each other deeply as we can.
You are more than I said before, more than merely
half of all I am.

Karen Ethelsdattar

Epithalamion

for Katherine & Douglas

The old custom was to scatter rice
at a wedding.
Instead I am giving you, Katherine,
& you, Douglas,
chopsticks
to gather it up,
to feed yourselves,
to feed each other...

& a recipe for a peaceful table
where you can hear your own thoughts
& listen to each other...
that first evening
I ever ate with chopsticks
I *had* to be successful –
the restaurant had no knives or forks or spoons
& I was hungry.
I ate in a room which was free of the clatter
of silverware
& it was the difference between
the uproar of city & the quiet of country;
I could hear the song of the bird
that sits in the tree of my mind
& the gentle thread of connection
vibrating among my dinner companions.

Karen Ethelsdattar

Which is not to say
that there shouldn't be meals aplenty
with hearty laughter
& the clatter of silver,
but may these simple eating implements
remind you also of the beauty
of quiet times together;
& the effort to use them
bring mindfulness of the pleasure
of the act of eating
& the blessing
of eating together.

*An Epithalamion or Epithalamium is a poem written to celebrate
a marriage or to offer good wishes to the bride and groom.*

Susan Spilecki

Now You Have Become One Pitcher Pouring Out Water From Two Sides

reflection on a Navajo wedding vase

A difficult trick, requiring cooperation
and grace, like a three-legged race
where you hop and kick your way
to the finish line. Such a pitcher is full
of contradiction. No more can you
say of the water, "This is mine," or
of the pitcher, "I." Now you learn
to say "we," take turns pouring out
on the dry ground around you –

for desert will always surround you,
awaiting clean water to awaken the green,
the flowering red and blue, from the baking,
cracked ground. Now you will practice
togetherness mopping floors and grouting
tile, opening doors in yourselves and leaving
them open, like the spouting lip of this
pitcher on each side. Now, man and bride,
woman and groom, you will cleave
like clay braided together, reaching around
to embrace. But first, you will need

to leave room in your day to pour out
over one another's faces, to quench each
other's thirst. And in your trade-off
for closeness, you must give up those
crabby mornings, easy freedoms, blithe
old habits. Sometimes you must give away
what you most treasure. you must give
water in due season. you must give to
each other, the world, in equal measures.

Alexandra Moss Zannis

We

How lovely rings the sound of 'we'
Now that we've joined the 'you' and 'me'
To form this sweet simplicity.

No longer am I just an 'I,'
Or speak of ownership as 'my';
It's now to 'ours' which I reply.

Cathleen Calbert

In Praise of My Young Husband

I know why all the old men want young girls,
why the other old men love young boys,
for I see how they are like the young girls,
having whispered into your ear, my dear,
and stroked your Chatterton pale chest,
the soft bowl of your Botticelli belly.

I know why men leave their old wives,
wives their old husbands, why women love
their men, why women love their women,
for you seem to me masculine, then again
feminine: your almond eyes, smooth cheeks.
I know why mothers do so love their sons,

and daughters their good fathers, and why
a bed is a good, good thing (as are
down pillows, quilts, clean sheets),
why heterosexuals believe they've found
a perfect symmetry of difference, why
homosexuals believe they have found

a perfect balance of mirroring, why
young lovers like to drink too much
and make a drunken, careless love,
why couples always cook so much,
and our lips dip in that slippery curve,
why the rest can seem like nothing more

than a morning lie we tell ourselves
so we will leave our beds and keep
an interest in our professional lives,
why many must make a dangerous love
and threaten those professional lives,
why all lovers will give it one more try,

why we are finally willing to fail,
why we will still let ourselves fall
in love, why I, surely old enough
(a cautious friend kindly implies)
to know better, can think of nothing
better than the buoyancy of your body,

the great gift of your gentleness, how
kind you are, in love with me, and why,
with a spinster's age and weight of sorrow,
in white below the green of your parents'
weeping willow, I will take these vows,
knowing nothing other than our love.

Robert Miltner

Garland: An Epithalamion

for Mark and Margaret

September, I give you crisp apples, trees ripe
as painters' palettes. The autumn wind sings a song
of the equinox, music for the changing season.
October, I give you mountains, vistas, vantage,
the farthest point to which the tracing compass
    stretches,
each leg linked before arcing back home, the circle
    full.

November, I give you down quilts and flannel
    sheets,
longer nights and reading lights, good books at
    day's end,
warm mugs of tea scented with citrus and
    cinnamon.
December, I give you holly and spruce and yew,
cakes sweetened with honey, each day a ribboned
    box.
And out in the yard, our angels traced in the snow.

January, I give you golden pears, brown
bread, and amber raisins. The year grows new,
brings us to a full stop before we start again.
February, I give you silence, blanketed in snow
As woodfires dim, our shared quiet deepens.
Our boot tracks in fields or hillside lead us home.

March, I give you walnuts. We open them
like fortune cookies. They are like tiny boxes
in our hands, holding treasures, memories.
April, I give you raindrops on your eyelids,
a light mist in your face. We love the tumult
of thunder, lightning's crack, the laughter of water.

May, I give you roads to run, trails
to turn down, what is around the bend,
and over the next rise. I give you possibility.
June, I give you open spaces in which
to move: summer fields, mountain meadows, sea
shore's dunes and waves as ends become
        beginnings.

July, I give you ripe wild strawberries,
full as lips warmed in the summer sun.
How the long days linger, the light like a gift.
August, I give you a ring, and my hand.
Take these: we are a confluence, two hearts joining
like tributaries to form one river, a life together.

Jessie G. Grabowsky

from My Dream of You

To me, your voice is the gentle falling
of shadows in the night.
Your presence is peace that settles
with going of the light.
Your eyes are the stars that guide me
safely over the way.
The moon heralds your coming
always, at close of day.
Your voice is the wind in the trees
whispering in my ear.
Your song is the song of the breeze
which only I can hear.
Your arms are the arms of the earth
on which I lie to rest.
I forget all my troubles and cares
with my head upon your chest.

Gary Young

Dawn at Las Gaviotas

Everything is rising. Past the firethorn
and the crimson roofs the tide is in.
The small islands sleep under water now
and the nut hatch, house finch, the darling mockers
all sing. I hear the many voices lifted,
the whispered prayers of thanks all answered,
and rest well, astonished even in gratitude
by my bride's quick breath beside me,
so steady in this huge and violent light.

Diane Kendig

To Speak of the Whoa
that is in Marraige

One year later, I wait for my days to shift
to a lower gear, coupling like facts
and not like all these miracles I feel each time I turn
to find you here – though I plan to find you
at my fifteen thousandth turn
just as the world finds spring each year and reels
    from it.

I found it this weekend driving alone across
the Ohio valley: thirty shades of green and yellow
punctuated by the creamy commas of dogwood,
dashes of pink and white fruit trees,
and the magenta stops of red bud.

I wake to such color at our apartment window
these mornings since, and, at my side,
another surprise, your presence that I'd wrap
in my arms and tie with forsythia branches,
those long yellow reins as from horses running
faster and happier while I shout *whoa!*
but let them run.

Dorianne Laux

As It Is

The man I love hates technology, hates
that he's forced to use it: telephones
and microfilm, air conditioning,
car radios and the occasional fax.
He wishes he lived in the old world,
sitting on a stump carving a clothespin
or a spoon. He wants to go back, slip
like lint into his great-great-grandfather's
pocket, reborn as a pilgrim, a peasant,
a dirt farmer hoeing his uneven rows.
He walks when he can, through the hills
behind his house, his dogs panting beside him
like small steam engines. He's delighted
by the sun's slow and simple
descent, the complicated machinery
of his own body. I would have loved him
in any era, in any dark age; I would take him
into the twilight and unwind him, slide
my fingers through his hair and pull him
to his knees. As it is, this afternoon, late
in the twentieth century, I sit on a chair
in the kitchen with my keys in my lap, pressing
the black button on the answering machine
over and over, listening to his message,
his voice strung along the wires outside my window
where the birds balance themselves
and stare off into the trees, thinking
even in the farthest future, in the most

Dorianne Laux

distant universe, I would have recognized
this voice, refracted, as it would be, like light
from some small, uncharted star.

W. D. Ehrhart

A Scientific Treatise
for My Wife

The ancients thought the world is flat
and rides upon a turtle's back,
or that the planets, suns and stars
revolve around the earth in crystal spheres.

Thus they defined the universe
till Galileo burst simplicity
by gazing at the heavens with a glass,
confirming Kepler and Copernicus.

All hell broke loose,
churchmen apoplectic, and the renaissance,
and finally Newton to explain it all,
a scientific substitute for Adam's fall.

Not exactly simple, but it worked
till Einstein stumbled on some quirks
in Newton's logic, and explicable
at last evolved incomprehensible.

not good enough, said Stephen Hawking,
who proceeded to apply his daunting
intellect to postulating ways
black holes disfigure time and space.

W. D. Ehrhart

He's got a Cambridge Ph.D.;
he's looking for a unifying theory,
and he's covered acres with equations.
Amazing. Centuries of speculation.

Okay, I'm not a physicist.
But even geniuses can miss the obvious,
and I don't need a Ph.D. to know
the universe begins and ends with you.

Connie Jordan Green

Collecting Old Things

(after Cathy Smith Bowers)

When I see dust boil up on the driveway,
my husband's arm hanging out the window
of his ancient truck, I know how it'll be.
How in the heat of afternoon he'll unload
parts of old motors crusted with grease and oil,
time-worn remnants seasoned black as the soil
where he played as a child, as the ridges
etching his fingers; screw drivers with shattered
handles; sockets lost from a set; battered
metal boxes and splintered wood ones
musty as basements in July rains;
wash basins needing only fittings.

How his eyes will shine as he lifts each find,
holds it to the sun, cap pushed back on his forehead,
his spirit soaring like soprano voices
on a Sunday morning. How he will move
aside old piles in his workshop, heap
upon floor and shelves the new collection –
the broken of the world he will hold safe
against the day of mending, will hold tight
in the belief that all things have a use,
need only the restoring hand of love.

Ginny Lowe Connors

Open Air

Convertibles look great in magazine ads,
all elegant chrome and leather,
sunsplashed, new, accompanied
by paper doll people, fine weather.
But every time we ride around,
top down, trying to find the road
toward youth, hair whips across my face,
sharply slaps and stings and flaps
about my face till I'm peevish, so annoyed.
The sun is merciless, a glaring god,
frying the faith I set out with
or suddenly hightailing it while rain
rushes in, drenching us completely.

Each time we set out hopefully,
my husband charged up
with car dreams, the kind that sing
inside the hearts of men. I can't hear them;
the wind is roaring, bugs are careening
into my face, making it hard to see
the glint in Marty's eye.
That's usually how it is.

Ginny Lowe Connors

But not tonight.
Today I had my hair cut short, recklessly.
Tonight we celebrate summer,
drive miles through air that ripples
past like fine, dark silk.
He slips some jazzy music
into the machine. Notes of the piano wrap
around us, trail off into night.
Wind combs its fingers through my hair,
sweeps tenderly across my skin
the way water does, when you swim
beneath the surface of a lake
and the long, hot day
just drifts away.

Bugs, besotted by high beams,
don't notice me, so I lean back, look up
at a plane flying over the moon, at stars
beginning to blink. Scents of August
wash over us with the rising notes of a sax:
wet earth, grass clippings, skunk,
then something sharp and spicy
like fresh herbs, a pondish odor next,
and oh, Dunkin' Donuts.

Ginny Lowe Connors

Beside me is the man I know
I'll always want to travel with.
He's taking all the right turns,
he's having a good time,
and so, by God, am I.

Deborah Gordon Cooper

In the Dark

Lying beside you
in the dark,
I make of myself
a small boat
and drift away.
No matter where
night lets me go,
I know I'll wake
against your shoreline.
Each pushing off's the same,
across whatever distance,
the bed,
the city
or the sea.
Our hands
tied in a soft knot,
our arms,
like kite-strings,
keeping the way back.

Roger Pfingson

Poem at Dusk

Silent except the soft thrust
of the trowel as you work
the ground around the flowers.

Reading here an hour now,
a dry windless evening
near the maple, I slant the book

toward the light that keeps
the shrill nightsongs tight
under the wings of things

just beginning to stir
in tiny rooms of bark
and earth. On the limb above

a bee slips in one end
of a bamboo chime.
The action of humming in

plinks the chime against
another. In the garden,
you turn and smile

as if I had said your name.

Roger Pfingson

The New House Garden
Baby Poem

Last night we finished planting
our first garden here
and our biggest yet.
After tamping seeds of sweet corn,
zucchini squash and cucumber,
we laid a mulch of sawdust,
then watered long and deep
until the ground seemed to swell,
row after row of string
turning whiter and whiter
as the ground darkened.

By dusk we were done
and walked back to the house
dragging the hose, its neck
and head over my shoulder,
calling to mind the green snake
a friend caught and wore
one bare-chested summer
to make the girls scream.

Roger Pfingson

Inside, a bee bumped along the ceiling,
a flowerless antique white.
I finally had to bring it down
with a paper club of unread news
before you would undress for your bath.
I watched your belly ripple
as the baby shifted, five days overdue,
wondering if this would be
his last night to work between us
as if he were pulling up roots,
like a plant about to break firm ground,
pull out and walk upon it.

Kate Bernadette Benedict

Glimpses of the Body
In a Modest Household

Enchantment!
I followed my daddy
to the bathroom
and what I saw
so thrilled me
I ran out proclaiming
the good news
to a roomful
of aunts and uncles,
all smiling.

Glee! There
behind the bedroom door –
my mommy with no clothes:
a great tall precipice
of flecked skin gleaming.
O come here, daddy,
I cried, I have
such a surprise for you!
And he let me tug him
towards her
and there was laughter
and no shame.

Kate Bernadette Benedict

Shame came later.
I grew older
and the grownups hid
and I too was grateful
for long robes,
striped pajamas,
the purdah of Turkish towels
after a bath.

Glimpses of the body
became a worry.
At summer meals,
the rolls of flesh
my shirtless father flaunted
overwhelmed me.
If I came upon my mother
unhooking her bra
I ran from the room –
the afterimage
of her low swinging breasts
filling me with horror.
And when one day
she came upon me
as I dressed for school,
I clutched the quilt
to my skinny chest
and screeched:

Kate Bernadette Benedict

Go away, get out!
Isn't there any privacy
in this house?

And, Love, I am still
a modest person.
That's me at the beach,
camouflaged
in coverups of terry.
That's me at the gym,
disrobing
behind a toilet stall!
Why, then, do I allow
your thirsty gaze its fill?
And why, when you walk around
half-clothed
do I peep – incorrigible! –
and want to see?

Kate Bernadette Benedict

It seems a clean
uncomplicated delight
in the body –
in its surprises –
keeps upleaping
from the days of innocence,
from some unpollutable
secret spring.
Feel it now.
Aren't we blessed?
Such ecstasy!
Who do we thank
for this unasked-for gift,
this enchantment
in which our marriage moors,
this glee?

Rosemerry Wahtola Trommer

Life's a Beech

to Eric on our 5th (wooden) anniversary

"Timber!" And just like that,
I fell for yew, began
to pine for your arms around me.
But you were such a poplar guy,
could I ever be the one to stroke your fir
and tend your fire?
Instead of willowing in my own fear,
I plum decided to spruce up my act, take a Gambel,
branch out, and ash no more questions.
I packed my trunk
and took the fastest root I could find.
When I finally lumbered up to your door,
I said with a cy-press your palm into mine.
I know that you're a bit alder than I,
but that never aspen a problem.
You seemed to be of the same 'pinyon.
So when you said, "Will you marry me?"
I said, "Oak kay."
And apple of my eye,
I wood do it again.

JoEllen Moldoff

Two Logs

Two logs
side by side
holding hands
the way we do
each night
in bed,
to begin
the journey
to sleep,
head to head

the way we lie
alongside each other
knowing when to turn,
how to fit
knees behind knees,
arms crossing
the equators
of our waists.

These logs
you plant tonight
in the fireplace
bear our names.

JoEllen Moldoff

We watch them
settle down
to dream
the dream of split logs,

to merge with each other,
singing in crackling voices,
first solo,
then duet.

June Billings Safford

Morning Song

Morning lightly drizzles over our dormant shapes.
Eyes open, fighting not only the new day
now threading itself across our blanket
but the noises outside our window.
Then one by one you list them
by their song, the sounds
of the sparrows, the chickadees
the buntings to whom you listen
with ears that are decoders
of the dots and dashes of birds.
And so I too begin to translate their songs.
They say true spring mornings never
come up silently. They are listening feasts.
And when I finally achieve an awakening
and can identify one warbling white throat
you turn and your motion is toward me.

Lisel Mueller

Alive Together

Speaking of marvels, I am alive
together with you, when I might have been
alive with anyone under the sun,
when I might have been Abelard's woman
or a whore of a Renaissance pope
or a peasant wife with not enough food
and not enough love, with my children
dead of the plague. I might have slept
in an alcove next to the man
with the golden nose, who poked it
into the business of stars,
or sewn a starry flag
for a general with wooden teeth.
I might have been the exemplary Pocahontas
or a woman without a name
weeping in Master's bed
for my husband, exchanged for a mule,
my daughter, lost in a drunken bet.
I might have been stretched on a totem pole
to appease a vindictive god
or left, a useless girl-child,
to die on a cliff. I like to think
I might have been Mary Shelley
in love with a wrongheaded angel,
or Mary's friend. I might have been you.
This poem is endless, the odds against us are endless,
our chances of being alive together
statistically nonexistent;
still we have made it, alive in a time

Lisel Mueller

when rationalists in square hats
and hatless Jehovah's Witnesses
agree it is almost over,
alive with our lively children
who – but for endless ifs –
might have missed out on being alive
together with marvels and follies
and longings and lies and wishes
and error and humor and mercy
and journeys and voices and faces
and colors and summers and mornings
and knowledge and tears and chance.

Cassie Premo Steele

The First Moment

You hold her in your bony arms
and her blue eyes crackle at your voice,
the voice I fell in love with, the voice
you gave in love to me. As you give
her to me now, as you have been giving
all your life. This is what it means
to be a man: to give all you can,
in voice and body, heart and hand.
You gave her to me nine months ago,
a gift from your sea, and though
at times it seemed to me that you
departed for another shore, I know
now, as I hold her in my arms,
that you were there all along,
in her, in me, and will be, still,
after we are gone. We will be, still,
in her, your gift from my body,
long after both of us are gone.

Dane Cervine

The Perfect World

You worry about the children –
are they sleeping, are they eating well. I worry that
    the Universe
may some day collapse upon itself
that God is lurching about as a gangly galactic
    adolescent
unsure of itself in the cosmic scheme of things.

You worry about the finances –
will we ever have enough, what is enough, when will
    we know. I worry
that there is never enough time to think the thoughts
    that must be thought
that when the translucent window of knowing does
    appear
I shall be buried in detail and never see it.

You assure me that collapse is not imminent –
that all adolescents grow up,
that I never cease thinking so time doesn't matter,
that I've never let detail stop me before.

I assure you that the children can be trusted –
to eat, to sleep, to grow,
that there will always be enough
that it's whatever we have today and will get
        tomorrow and
that we'll know it when we know it.

Together we make a perfect world.

Deborah Gordon Cooper

This Bed

For more than half of my lifetime
I have slept here, in the crook
your body makes,

our breathing
mingling in the air
above this bed,

bought, in the beginning,
at an auction,
bidding more than we had in the bank,

the tall, carved headboard
like a treehouse
in a forest.

No matter how wide
our separate days might open up,

the night invites us
to this tender resolution,

falling softly through
the rims of dreams,

reaching, it seems
even against our waking wills,
for one another.

Richard Broderick

All Clear

After making love, we rise from the bed,
trembling slightly, as if from the aftershock
of an explosion close enough to blow us
out of our clothes, distant enough
to leave us shaken, though intact.
Gathering things scattered
across the floor, I watch you go
to the window and fold
the shade back just a crack.
Yes, the world is still outside.
Daylight is in one piece,
the houses across the street
remain standing. It's safe for us
to settle back into the ordinary life
we were leading only minutes ago,
faces composed again, unruffled,
like the surface of a pond taken
by a gale that came and went.

Marjorie Buettner

Twentieth Anniversary

Husband,
poet of architecture,
for twenty years
you have known the contingency
of my lines,
the depth of my designs,
the load-bearing beams
of my heart.
When you draw me out,
like the moon draws the waves,
I am plumbed then saved,
aligned in the give
and the take,
in the length then the weight
of your oh so expansive,
the measureless massive
home of your accepting arms.

Barbara J. Mayer

The Good Provider

He's not the type to send flowers,
loving for him means long hours
spent on a job he hates.
To be a good provider
he dies a thousand small deaths
daily, comes home to hear me
unload resentment like mail
delivered to the wrong address.
He isn't lavish with things,
offers small kindnesses:
the pot of coffee brewed,
the car tuned for the mountain road,
the hose placed with care
to water every begonia in my garden.

Wendell Berry

Our Children, Coming of Age

In the great circle, dancing in
and out of time, you move now
toward your partners, answering
the music suddenly audible to you
that only carried you before
and will carry you again.
When you meet the destined ones
now dancing toward you,
we will be in line behind you,
out of your awareness for the time,
we whom you know, others we remember
whom you do not remember, others
forgotten by us all.
When you meet, and hold love
in your arms, regardless of all,
the unknown will dance away from you
toward the horizon of light.
Our names will flutter
on these hills like little fires.

June Owens

Sunday Morning

And as you sleep, still wearing crystal crown
Of dreams and dreams, my love, I will go down
Into our quiet kitchen where the stove
Has held its warmth, one final flair of flame.
The cat who spends his nights with other cats,
But knows that people-lights mean milk and coziness,
Will skitter sideways over spotless snow,
Come beautified with snowstars to our door.
And while he weaves between my careful feet –
All guile and gloss, as only cats can be –
I will fix a platter of oranges and cheese
And grapes, a clatter's worth of knives, a book
Of poems we have read how many times,
And English tea and bread and anise cakes;
Then, silent as our little beast, but not
One whit as graceful, bring my feast of love.
And, slowly, step by step, I will climb up
And kiss you golden as a buttercup.

Robert N. Wilson

Deep In the Countryside

We lived then, you and I,
Deep in the countryside of love;
No stone citadel to shield us,
No vast mansion to pamper us,
Only a plain cottage by the river.
There we were alone and safe
In delicious erotic privacy:
Dense, anonymous, absorbed.
You made a world for me,
And I some stumbling words for you.
Journeys to that green place
Are rare now, glancing visits
Through little rents and tears
In the thick curtain of time.
But we are proud citizens yet,
Freeholders in the acres of affection.
The cottage door still opens in.

Dorothy Ryan

A Gala Occasion

Like two apples
left behind on the tree
we are no longer
lush juicy sweet
golden delicious.
Past our prime,
we are more like grannys
or maturing winesap.
Climbing into bed we joke
about my arthritic foot,
his bionic knee. We pray
the knee won't buckle
his pacemaker won't fail
my foot won't cramp.
Ignoring our bruises
we turn to embrace
and slowly, steadily, ripen.

Leah Furnas

The Longlyweds Know

That it isn't about the Golden Anniversary at all,
But about all the unremarkable years
that Hallmark doesn't even make a card for.

It's about the 2nd anniversary when they were
        surprised
to find they cared for each other more than last year

And the 4th when both kids had chickenpox
and she threw her shoe at him for no real reason

And the 6th when he accidentally got drunk on the
        way
home from work because being a husband and
        father
was so damn hard

It's about the 11th and 12th and 13th years when
they discovered they could survive crisis

And the 22nd anniversary when they looked
at each other across the empty nest, and found it
        good.

It's about the 37th year when she finally
decided she could never change him

Leah Furnas

And the 38th when he decided
a little change wasn't that bad

It's about the 46th anniversary when they both
bought cards, and forgot to give them to each other

But most of all it's about the end of the 49th year
when they discovered you don't have to be old

to have your 50th anniversary!

Kathe L. Palka

Afternoon

The children gone
to other houses,
we revisit all
we've known for years –
the touch of our skin,
the rhythm,
of each other's blood.

The play of sunlight
through an open window
forms memory.
And while the scent
of love's making lingers
in summer air,
these hours pass
as easily as our years.

Kristin Camitta Zimet

Permanence

It's jelly jars and mustard mugs,
humble and squat, outlast the crystal
to reclaim the cupboards, though fire sings
urgent around the rim when first
licked fingers ring the Waterford.
Decades of piling in the kitchen sink
nip at the goblets, sliver the Lucite tumblers.
The silver, chorus line of curving flanks,
and stainless, lockstep row of business suits,
disband, address unknown:
forks spraddled in the flowerbeds,
spoons gobbled up by sandbox,
knives gone fishing.
As for our china, bluebirds in Wedgewood
nest out of register:
three butter plates, five soup bowls, seven cups
perching on saucers of unequal size;
a creamer, but the sugar bowl is flown.
Runners of Irish lace lying flat out
past bleach and darning have outrun
their placemats. Likewise our friends
thin out, unpair: love itself seems
a discontinued pattern.
Four children gone, straining the backs
of the pushed-out chairs,
we sit, a little wobbly,
down to a tag-end table that recalls
our first make-do. I raise
my jar up to your mug again: to us.

Norbert Krapf

The Riddle of Three Words

When you think
you have found
the right person
to say them to

you must make sure
you mean them
with all your life
and have earned
the right to say them.

You must also wonder
if the other will
believe and accept them.

Mere volume will not
convince either of you.

If you hear them
said to you
you must wonder
if they are truly meant,
if you are indeed
the one for whom
they are intended,
if you deserve them,
and exactly what they mean.

Norbert Krapf

If these conditions
are all satisfied
and you can say
and receive them
in all faith

they will seem
the most beautiful
short poem
in any language

and you will pray
you may say
and hear it
every day
the rest
of your life.

About the Contributors

Kate Bernadette Benedict's poetry has appeared in literary magazines and anthologies since 1980. Among her publication credits are *Kalliope, Slant, Rhino, Thema,* and *The American Voice,* as well as various online journals. Benedict, who lives in New York City, has worked in book publishing and finance. She is a moderator for *Eratosphere,* the poetry web forum.

Wendell Berry has won many awards for his writing, and is prolific in several genres: poetry, essays and fiction. Berry's poetry reflects his concerns about farming, community and living with the natural rhythms of the earth. *The Selected Poems of Wendell Berry* (Counterpoint Press, 1998) is one of his notable collections of poetry.

Richard Broderick's collection of poems, *Woman Lake,* is published by New Rivers Press. His work has been nominated for the Pushcart Prize, and has received the International Merit Award from The Atlanta Review. His poems have appeared in journals such as *Prairie Schooner, The Laurel Review,* and others. Broderick lives in St. Paul, Minnesota, where he co-edits *The Great River Review*.

Andrea Hollander Budy, an award-winning poet, is the author of two collections of poems: *House Without a Dreamer* (StoryLine Press, 1993), which won the Nicholas Roerich Poetry Prize, and *The*

Other Life (Story Line Press, 2001), as well as three prize-winning chapbooks. Her poems and essays have appeared in publications such as *Poetry*, *The Georgia Review*, and *Creative Nonfiction*. She lives in Mountain View, Arkansas, and is the Writer-in-Residence at Lyon College.

Marjorie Buettner's poetry has been published in numerous journals in the United States and in the United Kingdom. Buettner has won numerous awards for her poetry, including awards from the Florida Poetry Association, the Arizona Poetry Association and first place in the World Haiku Club's New Year's Eve Haibun.

Cathleen Calbert is the author of two books of poetry: *Lessons in Space* (University Press of Florida, 1997) and *Bad Judgment* (Sarabande Books, 1999). Her poems have appeared in a number of publications, including *The Best American Poetry 1995*, *MS.*, *The Nation*, and *The Pushcart Prize 2001*. She teaches at Rhode Island College.

Dane Cervine lives with his wife and two children in Santa Cruz, California, where he directs a Child & Family Mental Health Clinic. His poetry has appeared recently in such publications as *Quarry West*, *Porter Gulch Review*, *Old Red Kimono*, *Lucid Stone*, *The Haight Ashbury Literary Review* and others.

Krista Clercx is a high school English teacher in the Twin Cities.

Ginny Lowe Connors teaches English in West Hartford, Connecticut. Her poems have appeared in various magazines and anthologies, and have won a number of awards. Connors is the editor of *Essential Love* (Poetworks / Grayson Books, 2000), a collection of poems about parents and children.

Deborah Gordon Cooper has been published in a number of literary journals and anthologies. Recently two of her chapbooks have won awards. Cooper uses poetry in her work as a hospital chaplain and has conducted workshops on the interfacing of poetry and spirituality. She and her husband Joel, a fine-art screenprinter, have exhibited their collaborative images throughout Minnesota

W. D. Ehrhart is the author or editor of 18 books of poetry and prose, including *Beautiful Wreckage: New & Selected Poems*. He lives in Philadelphia with his wife Anne and daughter Leela.

Karen Ethelsdattar is a poet and liturgist whose work has appeared in many magazines. In addition, her work has been published in Starhawk's book *The Spiral Dance*, the anthology *Christmas Blues* and the

Papier Mache Press anthologies *If I had my life to live over I would pick more daisies* and *At Our Core: Women Writing about Power.*

Alice Friman's last book, *Zoo* (University of Arkansas Press, 1999) won the Ezra Pound Poetry Award from Truman State University. Published in twelve countries and anthologized widely, she has won fellowships from the Arts Council of Indianapolis and the Indiana Arts Commission. She was named to the 2001-2002 Georgia Poetry Circuit.

Leah Furnas and her husband Tom, who have been married for forty-eight years, live on the Oregon coast. *The Beacon, Voices in Winter Rain,* and *The Oregon Poetry Anthology of Prizewinning Poems* are among the publications in which her poems and essays have appeared. Furnas is working on a collection of stories for her memoir, *The Junk Drawer.*

Jessie G. Grabowsky, born in 1916 in Bellows Falls, Vermont, started writing short stories at age six and is still writing. Later she moved to New York City and went to New York University. She and her husband Harry have been married for close to 70 years. They have four children, nine grandchildren and six great grandchildren.

Connie Jordan Green lives on a farm in East Tennessee with her husband of 43 years. She writes poetry, a newspaper column, and novels and stories for young people. One novel was an ALA Best Books for Young Adults, another a Notable 1992 Children's Trade Book in the Field of Social Studies. Her poetry has appeared in more than 25 journals and publications.

Robert Hardy lives with his wife and two sons in Northfield, Minnesota. His poetry has appeared in the anthologies *33 Minnesota Poets* (Nodin Press 2000) and *Essential Love: Poems About Mothers and Fathers, Daughters and Sons* (Poetworks, Grayson Books, 2000). He works as a public school teacher and freelance writer.

Diane Kendig is a writer, translator, and teacher whose poems have appeared in journals and three chapbooks, most recently, *Greatest Hits, 1978-2000*. A recipient of two Ohio Arts Council Fellowships in Poetry, she has been married over 17 years to Paul Beauvais. About her poem, Kendig says, "I wrote this poem in reaction to two poems on adultery, one by Anne Sexton and the other by Robert Lowell, who were in turn responding to the Roman poet, Catullus. All three of their poems were entitled "To Speake of the Woe That Is in Marriage."

X.J. Kennedy's poems appear in Bartlett's Familiar Quotations. More than three million students have used his textbooks, including *An Introduction to Poetry* (tenth edition, with Dana Gioia, Longman, 2002). *Exploding Gravy* (Little, Brown, 2002) is the latest of eighteen books for children. He lives in Lexington, Massachusetts. The poem included here was written for a couple who married during the week after the terrorist attacks of September 11, 2001.

Norbert Krapf is the author of ten poetry collections, including *Bittersweet Along the Expressway* and *The Country I Come From*. Winner of the Lucille Medwick Memorial Award from the Poetry Society of America, he directs the C.W. Post Poetry Center of Long Island University.

Dorianne Laux has worked as a gas station manager, a sanatorium cook, a maid, and a donut holer. Her poetry collections include *Awake*, *What We Carry*, and *Smoke* (all published by BOA editions).

Barbara J. Mayer is a Mooresville, North Carolina poet and writer whose work has appeared in many journals and anthologies including *Atlanta Review*, *Crucible*, *Iowa Woman*, and *Earth and Soul*. Mount Olive College Press recently published her poetry collection, *Peacock*.

Robert Miltner is assistant professor of English at Kent State University. He is the author of four poetry chapbooks: *On the Off Ramp* (Implosion Press), *The Seamless Serial House* (Pudding House), *Against the Simple* (Kent State University Press), and *Ghost of a Chance* (Zygote Press). Miltner's work has twice been nominated for a Pushcart Prize.

Jo Ellen Moldoff, a recently retired school counselor, has been writing poetry for many years, and has given readings in New York with the Down River Poets. She now lives on Orcas Island, off the Washington coast, with her artist/poet husband and is active in the writing community of the island.

Lisel Mueller's books of poetry include *The Private Life* (LSU Press, 1976), *Waving From the Shore: Poems* (LSU Press, 1989), and *Alive Together: New & Selected Poems* (LSU Press, 1996). Her work appears in numerous magazines, literary journals and anthologies.

June Owens, originally trained as a classical singer, has written poems, book reviews and nonfiction, which have appeared widely in journals and anthologies. She is the recipient of numerous awards, among them a Prospect Press First Poetry Book Award for her 1999 collection, *TreeLine*.

Kathe L. Palka lives in New Jersey with her husband and their two sons. A co-editor of *The Higginsville Reader*, she tutors and trains tutors for Literacy Volunteers of America, and serves as deacon at the local Reformed Church. Her poems have appeared in many journals and magazines.

Roger Pfingston, a retired teacher of English and photography, published some of his first poems in *The New York Times* in the early 1960's. He is the recipient of a poetry fellowship from the National Endowment for the Arts and two PEN Syndicated Fiction Awards. His chapbook, *Singing to the Garden*, was recently published by Parallel Press.

Marge Piercy has written over a dozen books of poetry as well as over a dozen novels. Born in Detroit, she has lived in Chicago, Boston, Paris, San Francisco, and New York. She now resides in Cape Cod with her husband, Ira Wood. Much of Piercy's writing reflects her work as a political activist and her interest in the women's movement.

Fran Portley is a poet and painter. Her poems are published in *When I Am an Old Woman* and *Pick More Daisies*, two successful anthologies, and in numerous magazines. She studied under Robert Pinsky and she teaches poetry workshops for adults and children.

Dorothy Ryan is a poet and teacher whose poems have appeared in *Black Buzzard Review* and *Paterson Literary Review*, among other journals. Ryan and her husband, Mike, have been married since 1970.

June Billings Safford's poems have been published in literary journals such as *Outerbridge, Kalliope, The Paterson Literary Review* and in anthologies *From Seed Bed to Harvest, Passionate Hearts, Essential Love,* and *Fit at Forty.* She is a former English/creative writing teacher in Bozeman, Montana. Safford enjoys reading and writing poetry, spending time with her family, and painting.

Shoshauna Shy's poems have appeared in *Poetry Northwest, the Comstock Review,* on *Poetry Daily* and elsewhere. She is the author of *Souped-Up on the Must-Drive Syndrome,* a chapbook released in 2000 by Pudding House Publications and *Slide into Light: Poems of the Brighter Moments* released in 2001 by Moon Journal Press.

Susan Spilecki teaches writing and literature at Emerson College and Northeastern University. Her poetry has appeared in *Quarterly West, Ekphrasis,* and *Phoebe,* and has been nominated for the Pushcart Prize. She received a grant from the Vogelstein Foundation for a work in progress entitled *Body Blues.*

Cassie Premo Steele is a poet and writer living in Columbia, South Carolina. Her books focus on the themes of trauma and healing, the sacred power of women's bodies, and the connections between motherhood and mythology.

Rosemerry Wahtola Trommer lives in the San Miguel River canyon near Telluride, Colorado, where she is a hiker, skier, and optimist. Her poetry books include *Lunaria* and *If You Listen: Poetry and Photographs of the San Juan Mountains*. She also edited *Charity: True Stories of Giving and Receiving*. Trommer directs the Telluride Writers Guild.

Mike Wiegand, a Seattle native, has published poetry and fiction in various print and online journals. He works as a corporate executive speechwriter and freelance business author. Wiegand has two children, Sean and Rachel, and is married to his soulmate and the love of his life, Debra Jeanne, who said, "Yes!"

Robert N. Wilson, a poet and essayist, is professor emeritus of sociology at the University of North Carolina. His several books include *Man Made Plain*, *The Writer as Social Seer*, and *Experiencing Creativity*. He has contributed poems to a variety of magazines, including *Harvard Magazine* and *Asheville Poetry Review*.

Gary Young is a poet, artist and editor of the Green-house Review Press. His books include *Hands, The Dream of a Moral Life* and *Days*. A recent book, *Braver Deeds*, won the Peregrine Smith Poetry Prize. His newest book is *No Other Life*. Young's print work is represented in many collections, including the Museum of Modern Art and the Getty Center for the Arts.

Alexandra Moss Zannis was born in Indiana, lived in New York for numerous years, and now resides in Miami, where she is secretary/treasury of the Association of Florida Poets. Her work has been published in various poetry magazines. A poetry collection Zannis published is entitled *The Open Wound and Other Scars*.

Kristin Camitta Zimet's first collection of poems, *Take in My Arms the Dark*, was published in 1999. She is Associate Editor for Sow's Ear Poetry Review and helped found the Appalachian Center for Poets and Writers. She works as a nature interpreter in the Shenandoah Valley of Virginia.

Acknowledgements

Kate Bernadette Benedict: "Glimpses of the Body in a
Modest Household" first appeared in *Slant*, 1987, and is
reprinted with permission of the author.

Wendell Berry: "Our Children Coming of Age" was first
published in *The Selected Poems of Wendell Berry* by
Wendell Berry, copyright © 1998 by Wendell Berry, and is
reprinted by permission of Counterpoint Press, a member
of Perseus Books, L.L.C.

Richard Broderick: "All Clear" is published here for the
first time by permission of the author.

Andrea Hollander Budy: "Wedding Poem" is published here
for the first time by permission of the author.

Marjorie Buettner: "Twentieth Anniversary" is published
here for the first time by permission of the author.

Cathleen Calbert: "In Praise of My Young Husband" first
appeared in *The Paris Review*, summer, 1994; was reprinted
in *Bad Judgment* (Sarabande Books, 1999) and appears
here by permission of the author.

Dane Cervine: "The Perfect World" is published here for
the first time by permission of the author.

Krista Clercx: "Wedding Day" is published here for the first
time by permission of the author.

Diane Kendig: "To Speak of the Whoa That is in Marriage" first appeared in *Contemporary Verse Two* and is reprinted here by permission of the author.

X. J. Kennedy: "For a Wedding in a Week of Devastation" first appeared in *NorthEast*, of *The Hartford Courant*, October 23, 2001 and is published here by permission of the author.

Norbert Krapf: "The Riddle of Three Words" first appeared in *Family Celebrations*, ed. by June Cotner, Andrews McNeel Publishing, Kansas City, 1999, and is reprinted here by permission of the author.

Dorianne Laux: "As It Is" © 1994 by Dorianne Laux, is reprinted from *What We Carry, Poems by Dorianne Laux*, with the permission of BOA Editions, Ltd.

Barbara J. Mayer: "The Good Provider" first appeared in *A Carolina Literary Companion*, 1991 and is reprinted here by permission of the author.

Robert Miltner: "Garland: An Epithalamion" is published here for the first time by permission of the author.

Jo Ellen Moldoff: "Two Logs" is published here for the first time by permission of the author.

Lisel Mueller: "Alive Together" is reprinted by permission of Louisiana State University Press from *Alive Together*, by Lisel Mueller. Copyright © 1996 by Lisel Mueller.

June Owens: "Sunday Morning" first appeared in *Prize Poems of the National Federation of State Poetry Societies*, 1993; next appeared in *Anthology Eighteen*, Florida State Poets Association, Inc. Melbourne, 2,000, and is reprinted here by permission of the author.

Kathe L. Palka: "Afternoon" is published here for the first time by permission of the author.

Roger Pfingston: "Poem at Dusk," which first appeared in *Snowy Egret*, spring, 1999, and "The New House Garden Baby Poem," which first appeared in *Nesting*, Sparrow Press, West Lafayette, Indiana, 1978, are reprinted here by permission of the author.

Marge Piercy: "The Chuppah" is reprinted from *The Art of Blessing the Day* by Marge Piercy, copyright © 1999 by Middlemarsh, Inc. and used by permission of Alfred A. Knopf, a division of Random House, Inc.

Fran Portley: "Heart Over Head" is published here for the first time by permission of the author.

Dorothy Ryan: "A Gala Occasion" is published here for the first time by permission of the author.

June Billings Safford: "Morning Song" first appeared in *Yokoi*, summer, 1990, and is reprinted here by permission of the author.

Shoshauna Shy: "I Know Wichita, Kansas" first appeared in *Slide into Light: Poems of the Brighter Moments*, Moon Journal Press, fall, 2001, and is reprinted here by permission of the author.

Susan Spilecki: "Now You Have Become One Pitcher Pouring Out Water from Two Sides" is published here for the first time by permission of the author.

Cassie Premo Steele: "The First Moment" is published here for the first time by permission of the author.

Rosemerry Wahtola Trommer: "Life's a Beech" is published here for the first time by permission of the author.

Mike Wiegand: "If Thou Wouldst" is published here for the first time by permission of the author.

Robert N. Wilson: "Deep in the Countryside" first appeared in *The Poet's Page*, 1997, and is reprinted here by permission of the author.

Gary Young: "Dawn at Las Gaviotas" first appeared in *The Dream of a Moral Life*, Copper Beech Press, Providence, 1990, and is published here by permission of the author.

Alexandra Moss Zannis: "We" is published here for the first time by permission of the author.

Kristin Camitta Zimet: "Permanence" is published here for the first time by permission of the author.

Index of Contributors